being still standing stones in wales

Here in west Wales we are lucky, for many standing stones remain; they lie tumbled in long grasses or rear gauntly in fields of wheat, whilst others dominate stretches of moorland and stand sentinel beside ancient trackways. There are some, smaller and less assertive, which are embedded in hedgerows where harsh banks of nettles cover them... whilst all else has vanished, the stones remain; they are in a sense, the petrified voices of our ancestors."

—Terry John "Sacred Stones"

For Emma Verene and Irving Revene from my past.

For Jace and Julia from my present.

being still

and waiting, seems to be a learned behavior imposed on each of us at birth. The standing stones in Wales embody this sensibility and more. I discovered these stones in an old picture book some years ago. Planning a walking trip in Wales, I decided to see some of them for myself. With a local map in hand, I would hike for several miles through grazing sheep, lingering cows, farmers plowing their land. I traveled down local roads overgrown with hedgerows that billowed and overtook the traffic. The weather was gray and moody. And then, off in the distance, there was a strange occurrence in the landscape. A thing that had definitely been placed there, and was at odds with the rounded and natural shapes nearby. Stuck there – stuck in fact, for over four thousand years. The stones are from the Mesolithic period and believed to have been placed by Bronze Age people, thus making them the oldest archeological sites in the world (Stonehenge is 2500 BC). After the initial sighting, it might be another hour of walking before I arrived. The stones were massive – some of them fifteen feet above the ground (another five feet below). Once there, the stone towered over me. Respected and protected by the community, the *maenhir* (the Welsh name for such singular stones) stood and waited. Other stone configurations didn't intrigue me. The isolation and singularity of the *maenhir* was compelling and idiomatic. It is not known why they exist or how they got there. The stories associated with each stone and the mysteries and dark sensibilities that local farmers told about them was fascinating.

I made these photographs to describe the silent presence the stones conveyed to me. I sat for hours with each one. Leaving was difficult. They seemed to dance or move before me. Each frame revealed a different personality of the same stone. As I traveled and continued to photograph, I found stones that were included in domestic situations such as campgrounds, backyards, or hedgerows. I discovered the people who were associated with the stones – landowners and farmers, who had proprietary feelings about their stone and how it had affected their life.

In making this book, I have tried to include some of the individual stories which date back over four hundred years. Other stories are current and told by the person being photographed or are commentaries from my journal. Tales abound concerning the stones' existence and behavior. Being still and waiting are sought after sensibilities in today's culture. The experience of viewing the stones had a spiritual and meditative component which is referenced to in the book's introduction. Literature is filled with methods and theories on just how to get better at our silent moments and being still. The stones are aged and silent. It comes to them naturally.

—Marcia Lieberman

introduction

An Antiquarian Investigates

On a clear morning in 1811, Richard Fenton, a Pembrokeshire gentleman and noted historian, knelt before an upright pillar of rock known as the Harold Stone and began to clear the lichen from its surface. He worked carefully and methodically, aware that he was in the presence of an object of vast antiquity and mysterious origin. He had already visited other similar stones, some of many such scattered across the fields and hillsides of West Wales, all enfolded in legend and echoing with history, but he had found few clues as to their purpose.

The Harold Stone is no exception to this ancient company. Standing high on the coastline near the little village of Broad Haven, within sound of the surging tides, the monolith is a tiny focal point in a wide landscape that stretches away from it in splashes of colour, green and brown bracken, golden gorse and the rich reddish-browns and blue greys of the plunging cliffs. To the north and south, the land sweeps round in two long, encircling arms, imprisoning the waters of St. Bride's Bay. At each extremity are the humped shapes of islands, Skomer to the south, Ramsey to the north, both often veiled in misty rain or the heat hazes of summer.

We do not know if Fenton was familiar with all the tales that are woven around the Harold Stone. It is said that on certain nights of the year it leaves its place and goes down to the sea to bathe in the waves, always returning before daybreak. It was once so respected in its locality that it gave its name to the parish in which it stands, Haroldston West. Country people would bow to it whenever they passed by and it was believed to have some power as a healing stone.

Fenton was in search of confirmation of a different legend, first noted in the writings of Gerald of Wales, a twelfth century churchman. Stones like this one were once to be seen all over Wales and, according to Gerald, they marked the site of the victories, a century earlier, of Earl Harold of Wessex over the invading Vikings. Each stone was said to bear an inscription "HIC FUIT VICTOR HAROLDUS, Here Harold was victorious."

After he had cleansed the monolith of the "minutest lichen adhering to it", even after digging down towards its foundations, Fenton was forced to abandon his search. There was no inscription. Whatever its origin, the Harold Stone did not mark the site of a battle.

Fenton rode away in disappointment and later included a description of his visit in a book entitled "A historical tour through Pembrokeshire." He also mentioned a number of other stones, or maenhirs as they are called in Welsh, including three in the south of the county. One of these, confusingly, was also known as the Harold Stone, whilst the other two were both called the Devil's Quoit. Together, the three were the subject of "a vulgar legend", or so Fenton considered. On one night in the year they left their locations and went to a spot known as Sayce's Ford, where they danced in the moonlight.

Fenton noted legends such as these only for their curiosity value. He was more concerned with discovering the purpose of the standing stones and he would surely have been astonished and delighted by the work of modern day archaeologists.

Clues from the Bronze Age

It is generally agreed that the majority of standing stones in the British Isles date to the Bronze Age, roughly 3000BC-1000BC. They are part of a long tradition of stone built structures known as megalithic monuments. The word megalith derives from the Greek word for great stone and reflects the fact that huge boulders, often deliberately shaped, were used to build a variety of monuments during the period from about 5000BC until 500BC.

The oldest of these, and amongst the most spectacular, are the huge communal tombs, consisting of a number of upright pillar stones supporting a giant capstone often covered with grass. Within the darkened chambers and passageways of the tombs, the bones of the dead were stored. These graves continued in use for many centuries and were the focus of festivals that perhaps involved ancestor worship, shamanism and ritual dancing. There is evidence that many of the tombs were aligned to the movements of the sun, the moon or other planetary bodies. Some were so precisely aligned that at key points of the year, such as the winter solstice, the light of the rising or setting sun would shine through a small gap above the tomb entrance and illuminate the inner chamber.

From about 2500BC, changes became apparent in the societies and cultures that dominated Western Europe. A new kind of pottery was in use, typified by large, incised, beaker-type vessels; copper and bronze implements gradually replace flint tools. Opinion is still divided as to whether these developments were introduced by newly arrived groups of people, known as the Beaker people from their pottery, or through increased trade or the natural evolution of ideas and technology. A combination of all these factors may be responsible.

One of the most distinctive developments during, or even just before, this period of change was the construction of large circles of stone such as Stonehenge or Avebury. By about 2000BC, the impressive stone rows of Carnac in Brittany were being erected. Gradually, however, the need to create such vast monuments seems to have abated. All over the British Isles, smaller, more intimate circles and many individual standing stones were constructed. Like their predecessors the communal tombs and the great henges, the circles and stones were aligned to the movement of the stars.

It is probable that the builders regarded the sun, moon and stars as deities, whose movements affected every aspect of life. It would have been vital to record and predict the passage of these awesome beings as they traversed the skies. This carefully garnered knowledge would enable the priests to predict the yearly cycles of sowing and reaping the crops, of animal migrations for the tribal hunters to follow, even the flow of the tides. They could also foretell the times when the strength of the gods waxed and waned, perhaps during the solstices or at the moments of solar eclipse, when the light was snuffed out and then was reborn. Powerful rituals may have been held on these occasions, to mark the periods when the world slipped into the cold, dead hand of winter and then was warmed back to life by the renewed power of the sun. Perhaps it was thought that the vigour and fertility of the tribe was renewed at the same time.

As well as the circles, megaliths were set up in rows, in settings of three or four, but often singly. In height, they varied from small maenhirs two or three feet tall to giants of fifteen feet or more. In some cases, white quartz was used, but sandstone, grey gritsone or igneous rock was common. Many of the boulders may have been glacial deposits, or became separated from the parent rock by natural processes.

Some were no doubt deliberately detached by human action. The shape of the stone also seems to have been important. A surprising number are irregularly shaped triangles, or are square or rectangular in shape, but this appearance is not consistent from every angle. As one walks around a stone, its aspect can undergo considerable changes. Two or three of the faces of the monolith will be quite broad, whilst the remaining faces are much narrower. The Mabes Gate stone, at ten feet in height one of the tallest in West Wales, is a huge block of laminated sandstone. Its front and back faces measure almost seven feet from side to side, but it has a thickness of only a few feet. It resembles a giant knife blade, driven into the earth.

Most maenhirs taper to a point at the top, which may be a result of deliberate shaping that gives them an oddly phallic appearance. This in turn has led to suggestions that the maenhirs represent the male and female principle, especially when they occur in pairs. One of the pair is usually taller, more slender and pointed than its squatter, more rounded companion.

In some areas of Britain, maenhirs were decorated with carvings of axe-heads, spirals and semi-circles, the significance of which is lost to us. In West Wales, these designs are absent, though the Devil's Quoit stone in south Pembrokeshire bears circular hollows in its surface that may not be natural flaws.

The majority of single stones in Wales were probably erected by small groups of people and may have been intended as family or tribal objects. They would have been taken from the nearest convenient source, though this would still have involved dragging them for considerable distances across the countryside. Most archaeologists believe that this was achieved by using wooden sledges or rollers.

The sites chosen for the placing of the maenhirs are often spectacular. Few stand, as the Harold Stone does, on clifftops overlooking the sea, but there is often a backdrop of rising ground or hills. Sometimes a valley opens out below the site and occasionally the surrounding land will have been carefully levelled to make a platform or terrace. The stones were clearly meant to be visible from a considerable distance away. Springs, wells, streams and rivers are often associated with them, with the long axes of the megaliths frequently pointing towards the watercourses.

It would be interesting to know if some stones were placed in landscapes that were already considered sacred, perhaps hallowed by the presence of much older monuments. A number of megaliths stand close to features such as the communal tombs, but by no means all of them do so. Perhaps the stones imparted their own sanctity to a hitherto non-sacred site, which would explain why some maenhirs are associated with monuments of a contemporary or later date.

Archaeologists have discovered traces of cremated human bone, even complete burials, beneath some maenhirs. Whether the dead person had been sacrificed or had died naturally, we have no way of knowing, but the builders may have thought it necessary to provide their stone with a guardian spirit. Other stones may have marked the burial place of a tribal leader.

It has been suggested that some megaliths were painted or stained with natural dyes in order to emphasis their sacred and ceremonial natures. There is at least one stone in Pembrokeshire that is still regularly whitewashed, though how ancient a tradition this is no one knows.

The most important insights into the purpose and use of the standing stones have come from archaeology. During the last four decades a number of sites in Wales have been excavated and the evidence they have provided is intriguing.

Excavations and Discoveries

One of the first stones to be systematically excavated was the Rhos y Clegyrn stone, near Fishguard in Pembrokeshire. This tapering column of igneous rock, almost nine feet tall, stands on a stretch of marshy ground. Nearby is a low ring-bank some three feet high, which Richard Fenton described as "a large druidical circle" despite the fact that most megaliths pre-date the Druids by many hundreds of years. In the landscape surrounding the stone, two other maenhirs are to be found, along with several burial chambers.

The excavated stone was set in a carefully prepared socket hole, which was packed on three sides with rubble consisting of smaller stones. On the fourth side there was a small clay-filled pit that contained two tiny pillar stones. Tucked away beneath the largest of these were shreds of pottery. A second, fallen maenhir was unearthed about twenty-five feet away from the first megalith. It appeared to have been pulled down in comparatively recent times.

One of the most remarkable features of the site was the large number of small stones placed in what appeared to be patterns of straight, curved or concentric lines. This setting lay between the two maenhirs and stretched in an oval shape to the north of them. A further puzzle were the small pits uncovered nearby, some with a rim of tiny stones, others holding fallen stones that had once been upright, but which were later concealed under layers of clay. Some pits were packed with a filling of charcoal. There were also sections of closely and carefully laid cobbling which, although it did not cover the whole area, gave definition to the oval shape between the two main pillars. Archaeologists believe that this setting indicates that the maenhirs were originally intended as a pair and not as separate features.

Similar discoveries were made at other sites. When the Devil's Quoit was excavated at Stackpole in south Pembrokeshire, over three thousand small stones were unearthed, arranged in upright rows to form a trapezoidal feature that extended in a northeasterly direction away from a large, silvery-grey maenhir. It is thought that distinct alignments once existed leading from these rows to prominent natural features on the surrounding horizon. At Ffos y Maen – the ditch of the stone – a cobbled area that might once have been boat-shaped surrounded the monolith. Other sites have yielded thousands of tiny pebbles set into fan- or d-shapes, often radiating out from the main megalith.

Were these features intended as sacred precincts around the standing stones, defining areas of special power where perhaps only the initiated might trespass? Or were the cobbles arranged in patterns that were in themselves significant and magical? As the sun or the moon set splendidly on the horizon, or as a star sprang into the night sky, was a life-giving force thought to flow from it along the alignments to the standing stone? We shall probably never know, but it is always fascinating to speculate.

One fact that has become clear is that many sites contained settings of wooden posts. Although the posts have long since rotted away, the holes that held them have remained. A circular arrangement of holes may indicate that a hut once stood adjacent to a maenhir, but it was unlikely to have been a dwelling place. Huts seem to have been built in isolation, one or two to a site and, if occupied at all, most likely gave shelter to the guardians of the site. Alternatively, they could have been ritual in purpose.

In some places, the wooden posts may have been the first things to be erected at the site. These posts were sometimes uprooted at a later date and their socket holes enlarged to hold the megaliths that remain today. There is often no discernible pattern to the postholes. At some locations, they appear to be scattered randomly, whilst in others they cluster in curves or semi-circles. There may be as many as a hundred of them surrounding a stone, or only one, as at the Devil's Quoit at Stackpole. Moreover, the socket holes vary in circumference, though many of them are large, indicating that they held timbers of considerable size.

The purpose of the posts, like much else about standing stones, is unclear. They may have been part of the pattern of alignments, they may have marked burial places, or were possibly cult images. Perhaps they too, like the maenhirs, were carved or painted.

All the evidence suggests that, for a period of almost two thousand years, these sites were in constant use as ceremonial centres. For uncounted generations, people gathered around their stones during the sacred festivals of the year. Perhaps offerings, even sacrifices, were made, probably the help and protection of the gods was evoked and omens were sought that would reassure the group of their future prosperity and well being during the coming year. The regular movements of the stars, the continued cycle of the seasons, even spectacular and terrifying phenomena such as eclipses and the fiery passage of comets through the heavens could be interpreted and might give promise of the continuity of life, the certainty of death and the hope of rebirth.

A Time of Change

Just as a period of change introduced the age of the maenhirs, so another time of uncertainty brought it to an end. From about 1500BC, the climate became much colder and wetter. The people who suffered this worsening of the weather had for centuries farmed their land intensively. Large tracts of woodland had been cleared to make way for agriculture or had been managed to provide timber for building. The soil was becoming exhausted. Worse still, without deep root systems to hold it together and regulate the watercourses, areas of countryside were eroded of soil cover. Peat bogs, marshes and heathland reclaimed what had once been viable farmland. Even the population seems to have declined.

The old sacred sites fell into disuse. The religious beliefs that had sustained them gave way to other rituals of worship, other gods. The timber posts standing close to so many maenhirs rotted away and were not replaced; thatch slipped from the ritual huts and in some locations they were consumed by fire. Bracken and gorse smothered the cobbled areas and the alignments to the stars were forgotten. Only the stones, weatherworn and blotched with lichen, were left, dominating the landscape, increasingly mysterious and enigmatic.

Ghosts and Treasures

Gradually, as most ancient structures do, they began to accumulate a wealth of legend and folklore, a mythology that dimly recalled their former life. Perhaps the tales began as an attempt to explain why these things were there at all. Ancient memories may have surfaced, stories of dancing and festivities around the stones, handed down through generations, retold and changed until it was the stones themselves that danced or moved from place to place. During succeeding centuries, as battles were won and lost and heroes rose and fell and became mythic figures, so they lent their glamour to the megaliths. How else could a stone rear upright out of the ground unless King Arthur had thrown it there from a distant hilltop? And what else could that boulder be but the petrified figure of a thief, turned into stone by an angry saint following an act of sacrilege?

Other stones are reputed to have treasure buried beneath them. One, Carreg Fyrddin, the Merlin Stone, near Carmarthen, toppled over and crushed the man who was digging at its base to find a hidden hoard. Another stone in Pembrokeshire is haunted by the ghost of an unknown lady in white who can reveal the location of a lost cache of gold, but only if the correct words are spoken to her. No one today knows what the words might be.

Several stones are said to mark gravesites, a memory perhaps of the burials discovered beneath some of them. A lover killed by a rival in a duel over a beautiful girl is said to lie beneath Bedd Morus (the grave of Morris), a stone that also acts as a boundary marker between two parishes. Or was

Morris an outlaw who lived in a nearby cave and robbed passing travellers? An alternative legend describes his execution and burial beneath the maenhir by an angry crowd of local inhabitants. Another megalith, long since destroyed, was said to groan aloud whenever someone guilty of murder passed by. When a man who had committed a multiple killing approached it, the stone split from top to bottom.

During the eighteenth and nineteenth centuries many megaliths were destroyed. Farmers were anxious to clear their land of inconvenient stones that stood in the way of agricultural improvements. Other people saw them as handy sources of building stone and broke them up or blew them apart with gunpowder. Many maenhirs were uprooted and used as gateposts or hedge foundations. Occasionally, a clergyman would order the destruction of a particular stone, offended by the respect that such a pagan object still inspired.

Such blatant disregard for the powers of the monoliths was not always wise. Earthquakes, fire, violent storms and even death might follow an attempt to move a stone. One man who foolishly destroyed a megalith, despite the warnings of his neighbours, lost all his sheep to disease within a year, and was dead himself before another twelve months had passed.

Respect and Regard

Whatever their individual legends might be, the stones have continued to command respect into our own era. During the nineteenth century, passengers sitting on the outside seats of the horse-drawn mail coaches that travelled between Cardigan and Fishguard would doff their caps as they passed the Lady Stone, so called because it resembled a woman wearing a long cloak. Within living memory, people suffering from warts would wash them in rainwater collected from the hollows on the tops of Meini Gwyn, the White Stones, three megaliths believed to have healing qualities. Other maenhirs in Pembrokeshire are still decorated with wreaths of flowers on Midsummer Eve.

For a small minority of modern day farmers and landowners, as for their earlier counterparts, the remaining megaliths are no more than nuisances. They stand inconveniently in the middle of cornfields where the tractors must carefully skirt round them, or they loom over narrow lanes where access is difficult. They cannot be removed however, as they are scheduled ancient monuments, protected by law.

The majority of landowners cherish their stones. They recognise the effort that went into the erection of the maenhirs even if they do not understand the beliefs that provided the impulse. The stones come with the land; they are part of it; they are even seen by some as a silent partner in the care and working of the land.

Two stories may serve to illustrate this attitude. Some years ago there was a proposal to remove a maenhir from the slopes of the Preseli Hills and to transport it to a visitor centre near Stonehenge. There, it was to be exhibited as an example of Preseli bluestone, a distinct type of rock of which some of the pillars of Stonehenge consist. Several farmers set up a guard around their stones, to prevent them from being taken. Eventually a natural boulder, not one of the maenhirs, was selected and was taken away.

The second tale concerns my own meeting with a Preseli farmer, whose stone I was photographing. It stood in the middle of a sheep pasture. I remarked on the ewe and lamb that were huddled in its shelter. "It keeps them warm," said the farmer. "They know that, the sheep. It stores the heat of the sun and gives it back. You'll always see the sheep nestling against it." He gave me a long, measuring look, as if to see if I might be trusted and then added. "It's been there a long time, that stone. I don't know who put it there or why, but they must have loved the land. They were saying, 'This is our land, this stone guards it'. And it does. I know it's there, even when I drive past this field in the dark. I can feel it. It's seen generations of farmers come and go and it will see me go too. It will still be there when I'm dust."

I think he had summed up the stones quite brilliantly. It is that feeling of permanence, that presence, which impresses most people when they first encounter a stone. The megaliths are ancient, old almost beyond our imagining, yet as the centuries flow past them, they remain the same.

The sense of history emanating from them is profound. For that reason, one of my favourite stones is Y Garreg Hir, the Long Stone, a huge monolith standing on the slopes of the Preseli Hills, which is part of this book. Approaching it, one treads an ancient trackway known as the Golden Road. Since the Bronze Age, the Golden Road has been a highway for traders, farmers, great lords and humble peasants. All of them have trudged past Y Garreg Hir. Fifteen hundred years ago or more, the Princess Marchell gazed upon it as she was escorted to Whitesands Bay, near St. Davids, where she embarked for Ireland and her marriage to the Irish Prince Amlach. Now, whenever I stand before it, it becomes a link between me and that long ago bride-to-be.

A Chance Meeting

It was that sense of awe that first led me to begin researching the history and legends of the standing stones. The more I learned about them, the more there was to learn. There is the continuing satisfaction of knowing that there is a lot more yet to discover.

My interest in standing stones also resulted in an entirely chance encounter with Marcia Lieberman. I was spending a day in Haverfordwest, the county town of Pembrokeshire, and decided to call in to see Tim, a friend who worked in an information centre there. I stepped through the door at the precise moment when Marcia, armed with maps, guidebooks and cameras, asked Tim, "Is there anyone who can tell me more about the stones?"

The next few days were hugely enjoyable. Marcia and I racketed around Pembrokeshire in my car, visiting all my favourite maenhirs. It was like discovering them all again. Marcia's enthusiasm, her eagerness to discover more about the stones, was impressive. I could see that she was deeply affected by her meetings with the monoliths. What also moved her was their relationship to their physical surroundings, a sense of how powerfully they inhabited a particular landscape.

Since that first encounter, Marcia has returned twice to Pembrokeshire, most recently during the winter of 2001. We were lucky on the third occasion, as the rain that had marred our second expedition held off and we were able to reach sites we hadn't previously visited.

It was fascinating to watch Marcia at work. She would usually approach a stone quietly, moving around it almost cautiously, as if establishing a connection with it. Then, when this silent exchange was over, she would begin to photograph it from many different angles. Then, when the camera was put away, there would be another period of contemplation. Sometimes we would sit in silence, very occasionally we would hurry away, as the light was fading and there were other maenhirs to photograph. This always seemed to be done

regretfully, as if Marcia was promising to return again. On the occasions when the landowners were present to be photographed with their stones, it was fascinating to watch the way Marcia teased from them their thoughts about them.

The images displayed in this book are, I am sure, not only the product of Marcia's encounters with the maenhirs, but also of a long deliberation afterwards, a refining of her thoughts and responses concerning them.

The images are powerful, all the more so I think for being in black and white. The lack of colour, the starkness of the photographs, conveys the strength of the stones and how powerfully they dominate their surrounding. That monochrome quality seems – and this is a purely personal reaction – to bleach away all the other influences that might impinge upon our consciousness and distract us as we contemplate these great monuments. For me, there is a silence, a stillness, about the images that echoes the feeling I have when I am in the physical presence of the stones.

And yet, as any image should do, be it a photograph, a painting, even a written or musical image, they also make us think again about those things that are familiar to us. I know these stones well, they are acquaintances of long standing, yet through Marcia's eyes I become aware of new things about them or rediscover aspects of them that I had forgotten. There is a dignity about many of them. The Trecenni stone, with a tent pitched next to it, is impervious to the incongruity. The Harold Stone, now standing in the middle of the lawn behind a modern bungalow, surges up into light and air as if escaping from its cage of soil. The whitewashed stone near St. Davids glows against its surroundings, an eye-catcher if ever there was one, pulsing with radiance against the greyness of the background. And for me at least, the mysterious, almost reticent quality of the Devil's Quoit at Stackpole, is reinforced by its depiction in these pages. Sometimes, too, an air of menace, even of threat, is suggested, for these maenhirs are not always easy to relate to.

Above all, what these photographs capture is the agelessness of the stones. They are what they have always been, a part of the flow of time, yet aloof from it, symbols of the very human and understandable desire of those long ago people to make sense of the world in which they lived.

— Terry John

Where do you want to spend eternity?

A stone in Wales.

from the book *Grapefruit* by Yoko Ono, Wunternaum Press, Tokyo, 1964.

Gateway Gwaun Valley 3:30pm

Cornel Bach, Maenclochog 4:35pm

Hangstone Davy, outside of Haverford West 10:40am

Trecenny, campground near St.David's 5:30pm

Harold Stone is said to dance with two Devil's Quoits. In midsummer, decorated with flowers, it leaves its place to drink and dance at a nearby stream with the devil. At this site, witches and the devil dance as well. Witnessing this event will bring you good luck.

Ffynnon Drudion, Ffynnon Drudion Farm 9:30am

Rhos y Clegyrn, St. Nicolas 5:00pm

Deep in the woods near Whit Church stands Tremaenhir. Foliage seems to grow every which way, except for the tree. It has carefully turned direction to avoid touching the stone. Depending on the vantage point, sometimes you can't separate them, but looking closely the tree has moved aside.

Tremaenhir, Whit Church 11:45am

Frieda Rowe is a hard-working farmer. She is windblown and weathered. When we approached the stone, it looked like someone sitting with their hand on the opposite knee. The sheep looked directly at us through the fence. This fence was built after Mr. Rowe busted his plow on the stone repeatedly. He decided the only solution was to move the fence next to the stone. They feared moving the stone believing that when a stone is moved it is "moved from it's source of nourishment." Local stories are told of farmers being maimed or disaster occurring when a stone is moved.

"I feel the warmth of the stone even in winter." says Frieda. "At first when I went to the stone, I felt ignored. Now I know the stone is there when I pass on the road. I can even see it from my bedroom window."

Frieda Rowe, Rhyndaston Farm, Haycastle 3:30pm

Druid Stone, Druidston 1:00pm

Druid Stone, Druidston 1:15pm

Maen Dewi is recorded as having "disappeared" one night when a local man took advantage of the stone's enormous size and built against it a *ty-un-nos* (a kind of house built overnight so that smoke would come from the chimney by morning). This allowed the owner to keep it and all the land within an axe's throw. The house built around the stone has since vanished.

Maen Dewi, Yard of Drws Gobaith Cottage 9:45am

Painted Stone Gwryd Bach, near St. David's 3:00pm

Lady Stone, Dinas 8:30am

Mabesgate, St. Ishmaels 9:15am

28

Prisk Stone, Prisk Farm, Presely Hills 2:50pm

"This house originally had no windows that looked out on to the stone. We have all climbed to the top. At night the lichen glows and is somewhat luminescent. I think it weighs about sixteen tons," Pierce Thurstan tells me as we gaze over the breakfast dishes to his backyard. Pierce is a sea master and takes boats out to Ramsey Island. From the kitchen window the stone fills up the view like a large pet sitting out back.

Maen Dewi, Yard of Drws Gobaith Cottage 10:30am

Maen Cilan, Abermarlais Park

Near Aberystwyth 4:40pm

Right here, the two sons of King Arthur were killed by the boar, Twrch Trwyth – part of an ancient Celtic tale. I had to walk quite awhile to find these two which leaned toward each other and then would bend away. The heavy mist kept them ancient and heroic.

The stone sits at the base of the Presely Hills totally isolated. Each side of the stone was a different temperature. The wind was very cold on my face as I stood in the field with it.

Glynsaitmaen 2:00pm

Harold Stone, Stackpole 8:45am

Longstone, St Ishmaels 5:00pm

Harold Stone, Broad Haven 9:35am

Rhos y Clegyrn, St. Nicolas 1:30pm

A white lady haunts here after dark. During the last century any traveler going by risked being pursued by her. She was known to leap upon their back and tear them with her talons. No one dares visit this stone at night nor even pass by it.

Parc y Meirw, Llanllawem 2:45pm

Clochog is Welsh for *bell*. This stone is supposed to ring if there is danger about. It wasn't shaped like a bell in the least. I heard nothing. The only ring was the traffic circling around the churchyard.

Maenclochog Church, Maenclochog 12:30pm

On this ancient trackway, the stone is a marker for beating the bounds. Here young boys were beaten to teach them where boundaries exist in the land.

Maen Llwyd Stone, Museum of Abergwili, Carmarthen 5:00pm

Cornel Bach, Maenclochog 4:15pm

Meini Gwyr, Field to west of cottages at Glandy Cross   11:00am

Llangadog, near town of Llangadog 5:30pm

The original gate to the field was blocked and not approachable – overgrown with thorns and gors. After a short hike I found the stone waiting. So alone. So content. In the background is Cairn Ingli – a famous hill of small stones that looks like a strip of dark slate rippling on the horizon.

Just beyond in the Gwaun Valley people talk about the stones moving about at midnight. I had the opportunity to visit one night, but I declined. I was too frightened to know the truth. I spent a long time sitting with this handsome figure thinking that it marks some place of importance.

marcia lieberman

is an accomplished fine art and commercial photographer known for her images of people and public sites. Inspired by an idea she inquires and explores with camera and note pad. She has a deep conviction and interest in people and what they make or do. Research and field study are part of her process. Past projects include how women politick with Geraldine Ferraro in the campaign of 1984 and Tehauna women as a matrifocal society with a commentary by Isabel Allende. Her first book, *When Divas Confess*, was published in August 1999. That book explored the nature of opera and the singer's relationship to their character. During her many years of teaching at the University of California, Berkeley, and California College of Art, Oakland, Lieberman has lectured on time and space, dwellings, representation of time passing, and the interview as a visual entity. Lieberman resides in San Francisco and passes much of her time at the San Francisco Zen Center where being still is a daily practice.

terry john

is a Welsh historian and a native of Pembrokeshire. He worked as a teacher in England for twenty years before returning to his native country, where he took up a post as Education Officer for the Pembrokeshire Coast National Park. Now retired from this post, he lectures in history for an adult education program. He has written a number of books and articles on aspects of local and Welsh history, including *"Sacred Stones, the standing stones of West Wales; their history and traditions."*

acknowledgments

This book represents the support and kindness of many people. I wish to thank Gordon Goff who saw the merit in this work and encouraged me. His guidance and enthusiasm lit the way. Years were spent collecting the materials and images. Along the way persons such as Frieda and Peter Rowe, Christina Edwards, Joan Carlisle, spent time with me in Wales. On my first trip to Wales I met Terry John who shared his knowledge and enthusiasm of the stones and continued generously to spend time with me on each visit. His insightful introduction gives a context to the work and a historical perspective. I am deeply grateful for his contribution. The designer, Birgit Wick, is a valued and beloved colleague, whose sensibility shaped the pages of this book. In addition, I would like to thank Jane Wattenberg, Amy Trachtenberg, Carolyn Herter, Sandra Phillips, Joanne Rollins, and Jordan Thorn for helping me move forward.

credits

ORO editions. Publishers of Architecture, Art, Photography, and Design
Gordon Goff – Publisher
West Coast: PO Box 998, Pt. Reyes Station, CA 94956
Asia Offices: Block 8, Lorong Bakar Batu #02-04, Singapore 348743
www.oroeditions.com
Contact us: info@oroeditions.com

Copyright ©2011 Marcia Lieberman, www.marcialieberman.com
ISBN 978-0-9826226-9-8

Production: Usana Shadday
Project Coordinator: Christy LaFaver
Color Separation & Printing: ORO Group Ltd.
Covers: 350gsm Moorim art card
Text Paper: 157gsm White, a matt artpaper printed 4c with an off-line water based gloss spot varnish applied to all photographs.

Design: Birgit Wick, www.wickdesignstudio.com
Typeface: ITC Officina Sans, Neue Helvetica
Map page 57 ©2010 by Terry John
Introduction pages 2-7 ©2010 by Terry John
All photos ©2010 by Marcia Lieberman

ORO editions has made every effort to minimize the overall carbon footprint of this project. As part of this goal ORO editions and its clients, in association with Global ReLeaf, have made an ongoing arrangement to plant two trees for each and every tree used in the manufacturing of the paper for this book.

stone index

The location of the stones are given by a six figure grid reference to Ordnance Survey maps of Wales.